Write On!

GREAT GRAMMAR

Written by Charis Mather

KidHaven PUBLISHING

Published in 2026 by
KidHaven Publishing, an Imprint of
Greenhaven Publishing, LLC
2544 Clinton St., Buffalo, NY 14224

Written by: Charis Mather
Edited by: E.C. Andrews
Designed by: Jasmine Pointer

Cataloging-in-Publication Data
Names: Mather, Charis.
Title: Great grammar / Charis Mather.
Description: Bufalo, New York : Kidhaven Publishing, 2026. | Series: Write On! | Includes glossary and index
Identifiers: ISBN 9781534550421 (pbk) | ISBN 9781534550438 (library bound) | ISBN 9781534550445 (ebook)
Subjects: LCSH: Authorship—Juvenile Literature | Creative writing—Juvenile Literature | Grammar—Juvenile Literature
Classification: LCC PE1112 M38 2026 | DDC 425-dc25

Manufactured in the United States of America

CPSIA compliance information: Batch #CSKH26
For further information contact Greenhaven Publishing LLC at 1-844-317-7404.

Please visit our website, www.greenhavenpublishing.com.
For a free color catalog of all our high-quality books, call toll free 1-844-317-7404 or fax 1-844-317-7405.

Find us on

Image Credits

All images are courtesy of Shutterstock.com, unless otherwise stated.

Cover – B Calkins, SpicyTruffel, NotionPic, VectorHot. Throughout – SpicyTruffel, NotionPic. 4–5 – Impact Photography, SLP_London. 6–7 – PR Image Factory, Master1305. 8–9 – Olya Humeniuk, PeopleImages.com - Yuri A. 13 – Karynf. 14 – vovan. 16–17 – 3d_illustrator, Yulia Raneva. 18–19 – Yuliya Evstratenko, PHENPHAYOM. 20–21 – Rimma Bondarenko, Andrey_Popov. 22–23 – Ground Picture, Iryna Inshyna.

CONTENTS

Words that look like <u>this</u> can be found in the glossary on page 24.

YOU CAN WRITE

Are you a book lover like me? Have you ever wished that you could write your own book? Well, I have great news for you. You can write if you really want to. Woo-hoo!

I am Professor Hoot. It is my job to turn great readers like you into great writers. Believe it or not, no one starts as an expert writer. Learning is all part of the fun.

WHAT'S SO GREAT ABOUT GRAMMAR?

Every language has grammar. Grammar is the system of rules that makes language make sense. If we did not follow any language rules, sentences would be a mess!

Grammar explains what different words do. It tells you how to put those words together in the right way. Once you know some key rules, sentences start to make much more sense!

WHY DOES GRAMMAR MATTER?

Even the best story in the world would not make a good book if no one could understand the writing. Good grammar is the key to getting your ideas across clearly.

The easier you make it for someone to read something, the easier it is for them to enjoy it.

If grammar sounds stressful, no need to panic. We will start with some super simple sentences.

SIMPLE SENTENCES

We use sentences all the time. A sentence is a set of words in an order that gives them meaning. Sentences have different parts.

We will learn more about these parts soon.

Every sentence needs someone or something that they are about.

Professor Hoot

Sentences also need to say something about that person or thing.

is the best teacher.

THE CASE OF CAPITAL LETTERS

Have you ever wondered why some letters are uppercase and some are lowercase? Let's get on the case!

Uppercase letters are also known as capital letters. They have a special job in sentences.

Every sentence starts with a capital letter.

If you see capital letters in other parts of a sentence, you have found some names. Capital letters are used for <u>specific</u> names of people, places, and certain things.

THESE WORDS ARE CALLED PROPER NOUNS.

MAKE SPACE FOR SPACES

When you write a sentence, remember to make space for spaces. You might not notice spaces when they are done right, but you will definitely notice if they are done wrong or are missing.

See if you can read these sentences. Which one is easiest to read?

✓ Is this hard to read?

✗ Isthishardtoread?

✗ Ist his hardto   read?

SENTENCES SHOULD HAVE ONE SPACE BETWEEN EVERY WORD.

PUNCTUATION STATION

So, that is how sentences start and how you space them apart. Now you need to know how to finish sentences. That is where punctuation comes in handy. Punctuation helps you end a sentence.

Different punctuation marks are used for different kinds of sentences.

Periods are for sentences that make a statement.

Question marks are for sentences that ask a question.

Exclamation points are for sentences that show strong feelings.

TELL ME MORE...

See? I told you we would keep it simple. I think you are now ready to make your sentences a little more spectacular.

fantastic

beautiful

twinkling

sparkly

Using descriptive words can make your sentences stand out.

You can use words called adjectives to tell the reader more information about someone or something. Look how easy it is:

I am an owl.

I am a smart owl.

I am a smart, helpful owl.

TRY USING A THESAURUS TO FIND NEW ADJECTIVES TO WRITE WITH.

...AND MORE!

Sometimes, a short sentence is not enough for everything you have to say. Thankfully, there are words you can use to connect sentences and add more information.

Let's use these conjunctions to tell a story.

Benji was late for school, but he could not find any matching socks.

Benji had to choose whether to wear mismatched socks or no socks.

He put on one blue sock and one green sock.

READ ON,

WRITE ON

Isn't grammar just great? Even if grammar is not your strong suit, do not let that stop you from writing. The more you practice, the better you will get.

DO NOT WORRY IF YOU FIND GRAMMAR TRICKY AT FIRST. EVERYONE LEARNS AT A DIFFERENT PACE.

A great way to wrap your head around grammar is to grab a book and see how other writers write. So read on and write on. Maybe one day soon I will have a book by you on my bookshelf!

GLOSSARY

specific to do with a particular thing

statement something that is said to describe or explain how something is

thesaurus a book of words that lists other words with similar meanings

INDEX